CO-PARENTING STRATEGIES
FOR UNSTOPPABLE MOMS AND DEVOTED DADS

Keep It Classy

RAISE HEALTHY, HAPPY CHILDREN TOGETHER —
BEFORE, DURING AND AFTER A BREAKUP

Monyetta Shaw

FOREWORD BY

Shaffer "Ne-Yo" Smith

Keep It Classy
Co-Parenting Strategies for
Unstoppable Moms and Devoted Dads

Published by EVANGRACE PUBLISHING,
The Evan Grace Group, LLC
info@theevangracegroup.com

ISBN-13: 978-0692099636

Printed in the United States of America

Dedication

For my loving parents
Michael and Linda Shaw ...
you are the wind beneath my wings!
and
To my precious children Madilyn and Mason,
whom I love and adore with all my heart and soul!

Contents

Foreword

By Shaffer Chimere Smith, known professionally as Ne-Yo

*T*he purpose behind this book is far more important than just being an artist or an author. I'm sure I speak for Mo, as well as myself, when I say that what's most important is protecting the hearts and minds of innocent children, ours and yours. This book is about preventing kids from being on the receiving end of issues and circumstances that we grownups create for ourselves. It's about state of mind, helping parents remove harmful attitudes and behavior that threaten them and their children's wellbeing.

Far too often, the most important parts of the entire puzzle are neglected, overshadowed by those "ugly new friends" we make while trying to deal with a separation or divorce. You know them – pride, anger and spite. I could go on, but I'm sure it's not necessary. It's these feelings, these emotional wounds that blind us to the bigger picture.

Suddenly it becomes a good idea to keep his kids from him. "Yeah, that'll hurt him, because he hurt me." Or it's a great idea to not support her or the kids. "Yeah, she'll feel that." These scenarios are too common, and it's sad.

Once you are badly hurt by a person, vengeance is all you can see or care about.

Finding a way to be civil, finding a way to communicate, is the last thing on your mind. It's all "HELL NO, I HATE HIM, I HATE HER!!" All the while, not even stopping for a microsecond to think about how much a daughter needs her father in her life, or how much it means to your son when Mommy can tell him, "Daddy got that for you." That means

something. Not just something; IT MEANS EVERYTHING.

We've heard it a million times and it's always been true: *the kids didn't ask to be here.* Why should they be made to suffer ... because we couldn't figure it out? That's not acceptable, we should and we can be better than that.

Speaking from personal experience, I know how hard it is to think about the most important people in the heat of the moment. I know first-hand how it can seem impossible, and Mo knows as well. Which is why I support her book.

We've both learned over the years how to deal with each other, how to be patient with each other, to compromise and communicate with each other. Full disclosure: I'm still working on that one! But I know that the love we have for our children will always push us to overcome anything that would get in the way of their happiness. This understanding strengthened the relationship we have with our kids, sped up the healing process, and allowed me and Mo to be friends again. The same thing is possible for you. It's just that like us, you and your Ex will have to work at it. And if friendship ain't in the cards, then pick something that can be, as long as it ends up being what's in the best interest of your kids.

I'm glad Mo decided to share the knowledge she's picked up during our journey. We're all constantly learning and working to improve our hearts and heads.

I hope this book opens some different ways of looking at and dealing with your situation. I hope it helps you come to a better understanding, that it'll stir more cooperation between you. I hope it'll bring more smiles to your face and the faces of your family. I hope you do more than just read the book, that you comprehend, process, and apply strategies. It's one of the most important things you'll do in life – be better for your children's sake.

I hope you enjoy and most importantly, we hope the stories inspire you to try different approaches that can turn things around for you and yours!

Preface

*B*reakups are sort of like the kiss of death; numbness, sadness, fear, denial, and rage all set the stage for dizzying confusion, gloomy days, and lonely nights. It's so hard to behave like mature, rational adults in the middle of all the pain and hysteria, but as parents we have to think of our children first. We must remember that they're watching – that they're frightened and depending on us to make them feel secure and loved during the storm of separation and divorce. Hearing that their lives will be different from now on is gut-wrenching for them, but when we step up and put their feelings first, we can ease their concerns.

The first step is to get to a point of civility with one another. Once there, we must find common ground (the well-being of our children), which should inspire fairness toward one another. Trust me, a little bit of patience goes a long way … you can even become friends again. I know it's possible; my Ex and I get along fine, and so do countless other couples whose relationships ended bitterly. It's possible for anyone who's willing to make some adjustments – to embrace new ways of thinking and doing things, especially when you decide that separation and divorce aren't the end of the world. It's simply the end of a chapter in your book of life.

My guess is that you chose *Keep It Classy* because you and your Ex aren't in a good place right now, but you want to be. You know you need the tension to go away and the bickering to stop – it's just that every time you think about how it came to this you get mad all over again. I get it, I've been there. When I was in the middle of our drama, I decided I needed to get a grip on my emotions. I found myself healing as I worked on my first book, *Bigger Than Me*.

Writing about my feelings in real time helped me get out of my head and focused on the heart of the matters at hand – making sure our kids understood that our breakup wasn't their fault. We needed to assure them that as far as they were concerned, their dad and I were on exactly the same page – we loved them more than anything in the world.

That is key for couples in crisis mode to remember, because children do blame themselves for their parents' breakup. That's why it's so very important to make the extra effort to build a positive co-parenting relationship.

Finding a creative outlet during your challenges increases the chances of that happening sooner rather than later. Writing also inspired me to recommit to my health; I started working out again at the gym. The renewed energy helped me shift my attention away from our breakup and on to becoming the best possible mom and role model for our son and daughter. That led this newly single mom to recognize my undeniable truth – that I am an unstoppable woman.

This isn't intended to boast. Actually, the acknowledgement of my unstoppable womanhood is accompanied by memories of all the pain I endured before landing on my feet again. It's the same pain you may be experiencing right now.

I hope the following chapters inspire you to eliminate the self-doubt causing some of your distress. Make sure you identify the root cause of the distress. Often a relationship breakup can mask hidden reasons for prolonged anxiety and depression. There's a famous quote by Wayne Dyer, "When you change the way you look at things, the things you look at change." Being solo again is an opportunity to practice self-awareness. For those brave enough to do some soul searching, all sorts of brand-new adventures will open up for you to experience.

Time heals all wounds. This isn't just an old wives tale, it's more like a time-tested truth. How much time? Well, that'll depend on whether your end game is about peace of mind and moving forward – getting beyond the current situation.

It's important that you don't allow any one moment to define who you are. As long as you are alive, storms will come your way, and you learn to weather them – to bring an umbrella to shield yourself from the downpour.

I don't claim to have all the answers. No one does. I'm also not suggesting that developing a positive co-parenting relationship will be a cake walk, because most of the time it's not. Still, from where I'm sitting today, I can state with unshakeable confidence that situations evolve, things do get better.

Introduction

*M*ost relationships start off the same way, two people madly in love with each other, people who can't keep their eyes or hands off one another. It's "my boo thang this, my boo thang that" and DAAAAYAMM ... I'm the luckiest human on the planet!"

Until suddenly one or both of you wake up to discover that things have radically shifted. You can't recall when the shift began, all you know is that the euphoria – the swoon you used to feel from the mere sound of his voice now makes your flesh crawl the way it does when fingernails are scraped over a blackboard. For him, the sweet rose fragrance no longer fills the air when you walk into the room, let alone lingers after you've gone.

What happened? Where did it all go? The love, passion, laughter and dreams you shared ... all gone.

You were convinced that your relationship was special, that it would last beyond eternity. Instead, like so many others its magic seems to have vanished into thin air. Now you stand facing each other, two fire-breathing dragons, pointing fingers at each other – blaming and shaming each other, hurling profane accusations and weeping uncontrollably. You wonder, *was any of it ever real?*

Most likely the answer is yes, the love you shared was very real. But we're human and human interest is fluid, always evolving. We should think of these changes as the end of one chapter and the beginning of a new one. Embrace the unknown blessings ahead, or block them clinging to a past life – the choice is always ours to make.

Life surely would be easier if you could make a clean break, chalk it up to a fairytale and call it a day. Well, that ship sailed when you became mommy and daddy – the miracle of birth changed everything – created a bond between the two of you that you can't and shouldn't break.

Like it or not, in this regard you're not a solo act. You're a team. The relationship between the two of you is over, but you are co-parents for life. The fact that you're no longer "into each other" is totally irrelevant. You are equally responsible for every aspect of your little person's life until she, he, or they become adults.

Come hell or high water, egos and hurt feelings need to take a back seat for the welfare of our children. Cool heads willingly acknowledge that kids don't choose to be parachuted into the middle of a grown folks' mess. This is our truth, the reality we bear as responsible parents.

The good news is, couples learn to set aside their differences every single day. We all do it for the same reason – because we love our kids and want them to feel secure, be healthy, and be happy!

While you are developing your harmonious co-parenting relationship, use the time for personal growth, too – to become a better person for yourself and to each other. It happens in countless cases, the way it did in ours. The wounds do take time to heal, but they will heal. You'll need to be patient with each other, and with yourself. Mistakes will be made, and apologies and forgiveness will be necessary by both parties.

If you're thinking that forgiveness is just a bridge too damn far, I strongly encourage you to get with the program. I can assure you that when you decide to form a healthy environment for your kids, which includes forgiveness, then everything begins falling into divine order.

There's no such thing as a strategic one-size-fits-all co-parenting formula, no magic wand to wave or pill to take. Sorry. It's all about consistently doing all of the healing work – that's how to move forward. Conflict resolution can't be approached with tunnel vision; you'll remain stuck if you try that. Each family dynamic is unique, with radically different personalities, cultural beliefs, and religious and political ideologies. Any previous exposure to domestic violence, sexual assault, child abuse, alcoholism, or drug addiction will influence decisions and behavioral patterns. Remember that there's no universal problem-solving formula. You must try many different ways until you find the one that works for your situation.

As you read this book, you'll find a wide range of co-parenting tips to consider, as well as self-development advice. Providing quality information was high on my list of priorities. That's why you'll also be reading advice provided by author and mental health activist Terrie M. Williams, psychotherapist Dr. Cynthia Grace, and Terahshea J. McCray, a fitness and nutrition professional.

There are no hard and fast rules, either, on how to keep it classy. Adopting the right mindset will definitely guide your steps. But keeping it classy won't be defined by the kind of clothes you wear, car you drive, or size of your home. Your career and zip code are irrelevant. You'll define what *keep it classy* means to you and your family – however you envision it to look, sound, and feel is entirely your choice.

What does matter, though, is how you and your Ex communicate with one another in the presence of your children before, during, and after your breakup. Our behavior and attitudes at this crucial time shape their feelings about themselves and future relationships. This is our opportunity to teach them valuable life lessons about love, friendship, coping with disappointment, and conflict resolution.

It's possible that some will find many of the thoughts and opinions in the following chapters to be a little off the beaten path, and I would agree. Problem solving is complicated, so it's important to explore as many options as possible. Every thought is included to offer you different perspectives on various situations that can help you achieve your desired outcome. In other words, remaining open to the other points of view is a productive co-parenting building block.

I've been very eager to get this book out into the world to help inspire parents, help families heal, and empower women. Holistic remedies, corny humor, spirituality, imagery, facts and stats ... it's all in here. I'm still on this journey with you – mind, body and spirit!

I'm really grateful for the opportunity to share with you some of my humble opinions as well as a wide variety of strategies that worked for me and our family.

Monyetta

*M*y early childhood memories are of racing my cousins barefoot down the street, slap boxing, and running around some of our 88 acres of land making up games where cows and horses and chickens roamed. Jumping and sliding on the hay in the barn was so much fun. I was a girly-girl tomboy who loved baking for my many Cabbage Patch dolls in my Easy-Bake Oven as much as I loved climbing trees. I recorded my favorite songs from the radio with my favorite cousin, played them back and pretended I was the radio host – and sometimes the artist. *I guess even back then I figured that a woman could do it all.*

My mom always called me a "country city girl." That was funny to us – and I totally get it now. I've always been multifaceted. I love the simple things, but my desire for more is what drove me to thinking outside of my box, wanting to explore and see what else the world had to offer.

I am Monyetta Shaw, the daughter of Michael and Linda Shaw, born in Greenwood, Louisiana (but my address says Shreveport, which is one exit away – and the Texas state line is 7 miles away in the other direction), to two of the hardest working, most loving and giving parents on the planet. I could write an entire book about how they provided me and my two brothers the kind of life that every child deserves to experience.

While many girls weren't being encouraged to step beyond the status quo, my parents were busy allowing and encouraging me to explore all options available to me. I took them up on that freedom to choose ... what kid wouldn't?

I was a good student, I played sports, and was the captain of the dance line. I became a cheerleader, dabbled in fashion, and flexed my showbiz muscles early, hosting talent shows in our family living room with my cousins and friends. I won beauty pageants and would sing, dance, and rap in those talent shows as well.

Apparently, it came as no surprise to my parents that I chose psychology as my college major and went on to earn a BS from Louisiana Tech. My interest in human behavior seemed obvious to them. I'm told that even as a young child I would look for ways to peacefully resolve disputes between my friends by suggesting solutions that made everyone feel as if their issue mattered.

Now I'm All Grown Up
I'm a single mom and I'm a Gemini.
I'm a strong and confident businesswoman.
I'm a philanthropist.
I'm a published author. I am a proud mother!

This is a short list of accomplishments and attributes that I am proud of.

In the midst of my pain I learned that time does indeed heal all wounds.

When my relationship ended, it felt as if a band of thieves had robbed the night sky of all its twinkling stars. The bright future I'd dreamed we'd share together vanished right along with those stars. My spirit was nearly consumed by darkness ... but it didn't happen.

It never happened because I had so much to live for: Madi, my sweet little girl and Mason, my precious baby boy. Later I would come to realize that it also didn't happen because I am a blessed, unstoppable woman.

I began compiling notes, reading articles, and gathering successful co-parenting strategies set forth by child psychologists and holistic wellness experts – and that's my short list! I adopted excellent coping skills that I still use to help balance the delicate circumstances unique to our family.

I'm very happy about my decision to write this book because I know it can enable families to create new bonds while developing an ideal co-parenting relationship. It's a lot of work, and there are many different paths to help, but you must always use your own truth as a compass.

Empowering women is high up on my list of priorities. In my view, women are the epicenter of the family and community. It's through the state of our emotional, spiritual, and physical well-being that all life force thrives! Let me be clear, this statement doesn't aim to diminish the role of fathers or men in general.

I've been surrounded by good men who are dedicated dads my entire life. I'm sure you know many as well. I was a daddy's girl – his little princess – and I knew it! I grew up running to my daddy for just about every little thing. When I skinned my knees I ran to Daddy, when I got picked on by schoolmates or teased by cousins and brothers, I ran to Daddy. My mother worked nights at times before she changed to the day shift to spend more time with us. When I was younger my weekends were "mommy & me" days and so much fun. Daddy cooked our meals, washed our clothes, helped us with our homework, tucked us into bed, and took us to bible study during the week, where we learned to praise God through song and prayer.

My daddy made me feel safe, valued, and loved every single day throughout my childhood. To this day I still run to him for comfort, support, and advice! My dad will always have my back. He is the one man on the planet who will always love me unconditionally, this I know!

I believe that every child should have a loving, thoughtful dad, one who spends quality time with them. A dad who seeks opportunities be a positive influence, help with homework, and provide guidance along with emotional, physical, and financial support. Although my children's dad and I didn't go out of our way to be spiteful to one another, our breakup was messy and unfortunately in the public eye. But I knew exactly what I needed and wanted moving forward. I wanted peace of mind. I wanted our children to enjoy every moment they spent with their dad, to be carefree. I wanted them to know that their place in our hearts is forever secure and sacred regardless of the change in our relationship. Keeping my ego in check, rather than conspiring with it to block happiness, was a major step toward the satisfying life I'm living now.

I understood how important it was to work on myself. I believed I'd be rewarded with peace of mind. I started to practice meditation and made a commitment to exercise regularly. I doubled down on my faith and prayed to God for strength, compassion, and healing. I stopped watching garbage on television and listening to music that assaulted my womanhood and my spirit. I hired a life coach to help me stay on track with my business goals and my life purpose.

There have been lots of events over the past couple of years; Shaffer married, and we're now a blended family. Our children have a beautiful baby brother and another sibling on the way. Celebrity breakups come with the added burden of public opinion insisting its way into private family matters, and this can automatically increase challenges – and traps we could have easily fallen into. Thankfully, we're mature adults, fully aware that our kids stand to lose the most; we weren't about to be pushed down that road-to-nowhere. Previously, whenever differences popped up, my response was "let's talk through it." I knew we needed to be open-minded throughout this journey. We have children to protect from the madness, and that held our focus and shaped intentions.

After all, we truly are in charge of our own emotions. I've seen what happens to people when egos go unchecked, and how that stifles personal growth.

Children can't be what they can't see. So wrote Marianne Wright Edelman, president and founder of The Children's Defense Fund. I fell in love with her quote from the moment I read it. "You can't be what you can't see."

Keep that in mind as you navigate through turbulent times. Pause to reflect on who you want your children to see when they're watching you. Will it be the two most important people in their lives behaving civilly toward each other, or strangers at war? However you decide to perform, just know that either of those options will determine, to some degree, the way your children will feel about themselves.

In the midst of your own hurt feelings, you must consider how you want your children to experience the world around them. Are you setting an example that teaches them how to love, let go, and love again? Will they learn from you how to expect respect and be respectful? I believe you can. This book is intended to provide you with information and ideas for choices that can serve your desire to strike a balance and be at peace with life's ever-changing winds.

Let's dive in!

The Sky Is Falling

Five Things Parents Should Do Together

*L*et's take a look at the world through the eyes of our children.

The transition during most breakups is gut-wrenching. Unfortunately, too often innocent children are swept into the darkest hours of our emotional storm. Our role as parents is to do everything within our power to avoid causing the children emotional distress.

We must remember that in their minds and hearts, the sky is falling – the earth is quaking and cracking beneath their feet. Their minds are frightened, confused, lonely, and fraught with despair. They see themselves slipping through the cracks, reaching out for arms that they imagine won't be there to catch them ever again. They no longer feel secure because they see their safety nets unraveling right before their eyes.

What now, they wonder, what now? If mom and dad fell out of love with each other, maybe they won't love me anymore.

In silent moments they ask questions of themselves and assign blame to themselves. What did I do to bring about this split? This is all my fault. It's because I'm bad – it's because I don't clean my room – it's because I won't eat my dinner – my report card wasn't good enough – I ask for too many new toys – I ask for too many new clothes – I talk too loud, too fast, too much!

They promise to behave better, they pray we change our minds, they weep silently into their pillows, they sit idly waiting for the world to go dark. While they're waiting, they become depressed and sad and vengeful. Over time their grades drop and they continue on a downward spiral, becoming more unhealthy in every imaginable and unimaginable way.

The longer children witness their parents bickering, badmouthing or slandering, or even assaulting each other, the deeper their wounds – the more soul-crushing for them.

It's never fair to leave it up to them to figure out the "what now" on their own. Instead we should act fast to ease their troubled spirits, hearts, and minds. It is our responsibility to do so. We must focus our attention on their needs and pour our passion into creating a new sanctuary reality for them. Regardless of age, children need both of their parents to assure them that our bond with them is unbreakable.

We must tell them – and most important we must show them, that where they're concerned, our love is unwavering and will always be unconditional. It's a pledge mothers and fathers should feel proud to enthusiastically co-sign on each other's behalf from the very beginning.

I understand how incredibly difficult this might seem, especially when you're hurting and trying to wrap your brain around what caused your relationship to end in the first place. But I'm also aware that most parents will take a bullet for their child. I imagine you'd agree that it's easier and less lethal to negotiate visitation and financial support with your Ex than it is to be struck in the chest with a bullet ... I'm just sayin'!

For the record, Shaffer and I didn't do everything right in the beginning either. We made plenty of mistakes, same as couples before us. Even now, we stumble periodically, but as we remind ourselves, we're a work in progress. It's important to us that we improve each time and our conflicts never escalated to the point of irreparable harm. Throughout the book, I'll share some techniques that worked for us and hopefully you'll be able to benefit from them as well.

Expert recommendations include the following:

- Both parents should tell all the children at the same time, regardless of the differences in their ages. Older children shouldn't be asked to keep secrets from their younger siblings; it sends the wrong message about the importance of telling the truth and forces them to relive the trauma.

- Take care to set the tone and environment beforehand. It's not a public event; it's a private affair to take place at home.
- Calmly explain your decision. DO NOT point fingers or blame each other. If you feel like you won't be able to manage this alone, you should consider a third party being present to help facilitate calmness. Think clergy, or an unbiased family member – even a mutual friend who loves and respects both of you!
- Don' t underestimate their feelings or their reaction to the news. Ask them if they have any questions and answer them honestly. What seems odd to you makes perfect sense to them, or vice versa. Our job as parents is to understand and accept their feelings.
- Speak with a unified understanding, take responsibility for the divorce. When we're being honest, we recognize that it's seldom a one-way street.

Bottom line: avoid toxic emotions during this important announcement. This is a pivotal moment in your child's life, and they'll never forget their feelings about this day and how you made them feel.

Unseen Scars

Do Not Miss These Dangerous Signs

*I*f your child suddenly lost interest in eating her favorite food for a day, would you think anything of it? What about two days, three, maybe four or more days? Would you chalk it up to maybe she's coming down with a little flu bug? How about if she's wanting to spend way more time alone or being way less talkative? You could be right about the flu, but you could also be dead wrong.

There is a reason that as responsible parents we don't leave small children alone in the kitchen near an open flame. We know they might place their hand over the fire and end up with third-degree burns! Just the thought of something like that happening on your watch will make you lose sleep.

Most of us are paranoid enough to imagine the ugly scar, so we use extra precaution. We imagine the physical pain a child would experience during the healing process. Not to mention our inability to escape the result of our poor judgment! Every time we look at the scar we'd be reminded of when and how it got there. We'd relive the moment in our minds-eye over and over again. The sight of tears rolling down little cheeks, fear in their eyes and agonizing cries would be amplified like some bad horror movie that we can't turn off.

We can't bear the guilt we'd feel either. "If only I hadn't stepped away to respond to that text, if I hadn't run into the other room to answer the phone, gotten caught up in the foolishness on TV, if only I'd ignored that meaningless tweet or snapchat video Facebook post or Instagram pic! If, if, if, if, if! But all the if's in the world won't erase that ugly scar and we know it! The very thought of our child hurting terrifies and shames us.

It's also why we guard against other potentially harmful events. We hold our children's hands crossing the street to protect them from traffic, we secure our infants and toddlers in their car seats, we cover electrical sockets and make sure window guards are properly installed.

We buy our boys and girls protective gear, helmets, knee pads, elbow pads, and athletic cups for school sports and other recreational activities. We warn them about stranger danger and we warn (no, we drill them) about drugs, alcohol, premature and unsafe sex. We know these things can cause them physical pain and trauma and wreck their lives – and it's just not happening, not on your watch! Right?

But what about the unseen scars? The ones that introduce mental health problems, which like a broken arm or leg, can have a crippling effect in other ways. Both kinds of injuries, if left untreated, cannot heal.

When separation is in the air, it's reasonable to expect children to express anger, anxiety, blame, and even mild depression. However, if the behavior lingers, you'll want to be proactive, especially if your child starts showing signs of the following behaviors:

- Problems sleeping
- Poor concentration
- Trouble at school
- Refusal to participate in favorite activities
- Drug or alcohol abuse
- Self-harm
- Eating disorders
- Angry or violent outburst (with frequency)
- Withdrawal from loved ones

Under any of those circumstances I'd leap into family counseling to get my child on track. There are many solutions available to help fix problems that arise from divorce and separation. All that is required is an open mind and the will to engage the solutions.

If you choose to work with a therapist, remember to do your homework. Your goal is to identify a qualified professional that you and your family feel comfortable working with. Don't do anything blindly. If your physician recommends a medication for your child, take the time to learn about any side effects.

Strong Boys vs. Broken Men

$\mathcal{I}$ believe that the happiness of future generations depends on what we give to them today. One thing I hope to see in my lifetime is a giant improvement in relationships between men and women. I'm convinced that major adjustments must occur in order for that to become a reality. I don't consider anything I'm saying to be uniquely my hope. In fact, I believe that the majority of women and men who've struggled in relationships want their children to have a very different experience. This chapter is intended to create a dialogue where there currently is none.

I've always had a healthy appreciation for wanting to know more about what drives behavior – what makes us tick. The desire to understand people and social dynamics is the reason I chose to pursue a degree in psychology in the first place.

Our brain is like a sponge, always soaking up information, processing and categorizing the data. All we need to do is think about the decisions we make or how we respond to different situations. Whether positive or negative, the choices have been influenced by nearly everything we were exposed to as children.

In one of his speeches, abolitionist and social reformer Frederick Douglass said, "It is easier to build strong boys than to fix broken men."

If by strong he meant emotionally balanced and spiritually grounded, then I couldn't agree more. But I think we can all agree that too many men equate manhood with physical strength and the ability to hide any vulnerability – to wear a mask that conceals their pain. Stony and stoic, that's "strength."

Heaven forbid a boy might show the slightest sign that he might shed a tear because his feelings have been hurt. When that happens, he's immediately told to "man up" and made to feel ashamed. Boys don't cry he is told, followed by "stop acting like a girl," which illustrates the inaccurate assumption that girls and women are "weak." Of course this sets the stage for young boys to feel (and act like) they have the right to dominate and control girls. I think we all know how that turns out.

The masculinity indoctrination wouldn't be complete without also using the "gay" accusation, as if being gay is some sort of an insult – less strong, less manly, less stoic.

This type of misguided instruction and negative stereo-typing is still far too prevalent. It's no wonder that adult men struggle to engage in healthy, loving relationships.

This isn't about bashing men, I'm in fact opposed to it. This is about changing the conversation to give boys and men the chance they deserve to experience emotional freedom – and real strength.

The reality is just because men are shamed into hiding their true feelings, *it doesn't mean those feelings don't exist* for them. It just means they get really good at suppressing feelings, which causes men to become depressed, resentful, and in some instances dangerous. Research shows that domestic abuse and sexual assault are strongly connected to the belief that "real" men are supposed to be powerful, dominating, fearless, and emotionless.

So yes, Mr. Douglass, I wholeheartedly agree, it is easier to build strong boys than to fix broken men. From where I sit, that begins with their freedom to express the most basic human emotions:

- Joy
- Sadness
- Anger
- Fear

Many of us are eager to do the right thing to improve the quality of our relationships with one another. The best place to begin is at home with our own children, remembering that mental health is crucial to overall physical health. I will always encourage our son and daughter to express their feelings freely.

Strong mind-shift movements are already underway. Organizations run by thought-leaders who work tirelessly to help young boys develop a healthy attitude about manhood are making a difference.

In 2015 my friend, mental health advocate Terrie Williams, and Madeline McCray co-produced the New Legacy Leaders Domestic Violence Healing Conference at Harlem Hospital in New York. The two women created a safe space for men to share their thoughts with leaders from several organizations.

Ted Bunch, co-founder of "A Call to Men" shared with attendees how they use the term "Man Box" to illustrate the collective socialization of men. The term identifies the limitations on what a man is supposed to be and supposed to believe. The organization encourages the freedom to embrace and express a full range of emotions.

Clearly we need to start early, by allowing our boys to cry, validating their feelings, assuring them that it's okay to be afraid and it's okay to ask for help. That's how we'll eventually break the cycle and raise healthy, well-adjusted boys who grow into men who understand how to value, respect, and protect girls and women.

I sincerely hope that both parents can appreciate the value of incorporating these suggestions into your co-parenting plans. It's definitely an important conversation to have with each other – and it's important to do whatever it takes to get on the same page. It won't always be easy, but it will always be worth it.

The Peace Process

Communication Tips

*A*ny reasonable collection of do's and don'ts for effective communicating in good co-parenting probably depends to some degree on how and why the breakup occurred. My original plan was to focus on women who'd reached the point of knowing that the time had come to move on from a relationship that had run its course. I think you know what I mean. I'm talking about that sweet dream – the one where you meet your soulmate, get married, buy a home, start your new family, and raise your children together under one roof. It's a worthy, beautiful, timeless dream.

By the way, many men want those things too.

But what if it doesn't work according to the plan? What if you're suddenly confronted with having to accept a new family lifestyle – co-parenting while living separate lives?

Emotions are bound to run hot and cold no matter what or who's at fault. Unfortunately, this blocks communication at a time when it is most needed for both parties. It's in everyone's best interest to get closure for the purpose of healing and gaining inner peace. Needless to say, where children are concerned the lines of communication must remain open.

Holding onto anger, speaking harshly to each other not only is a waste of valuable time, it also drains your energy and releases harmful toxins into the body that can set you on the path to life-threatening illnesses. Who needs the drama?! No one. You don't have to give in to raw human emotions; you can choose a healthier approach – come up with plans to release bad feelings before coming into contact with each other.

Keep it classy, and be creative!

Let's take the worst case scenario – you can't stand the sight or sound of each other, but you need to schedule visitation. You'll both need to make a commitment to keep an open dialogue about your children. Rather than starting with verbal demands and dismissals, you can:

- Use email or text messaging to establish parameters for scheduling visitation that both of you can agree on. Simply write, "For the time being, I think it's best that we communicate about the kids through text and email."

- Avoid using all CAPS or using red to highlight text; it's the same as yelling. Remember the whole point of going digital is to avoid conflict.
- Use voicemail, but watch your tone! Yes, sometimes just picking up the phone will cause your heart to race a bit. Take deep breaths beforehand, or reach out to someone who'll help you laugh...anything that can help you sound civil and calm will render a better result.

Prevention is better than damage control. Here are a few steps that can help avoid conflict and keep it classy:

- Be mindful of your schedules before asking or agreeing to dates and times to pick up or bring your child back home. Last-minute cancellations create additional chaos between parents and disappointment for children.
- Provide as much advance notice as possible so the other parent can adjust her or his schedule. You're caught in traffic or a meeting is running overtime or the trains aren't running on time or your bike was stolen ... WHATEVER, take a moment to send a text.
- Be adults, apologize ... and accept apologies. Remember, stuff happens. So be flexible.

- Identify a support team. If you can afford family counseling, go for it. Contact your religious leader, a "neutral" family member, or a mutual friend. Until civility is achieved, it may very well help to drop off and pick up the children at someone else's home for the visitation exchange.
- Make the courthouse your last resort. Whenever possible, try resolving your issues without legal intervention. Dragging each other into court will cost time, energy, and money that could be better allocated for your child's education and other expenses.

Do your very best to quickly get beyond the bitter phase. It helps to remember that once upon a time you loved and appreciated each other. Your children were conceived in that love. Knowing that will give them peace of mind, even if you're currently wondering, What the hell was I thinking?!"

The way I see it, there are choices. You need to make a decision, early in the process, about the results you want, about what's most important to you. If all that matters to you is "I'm right, he's wrong" then be prepared to lose sleep, gain weight, be sick, put your child's financial support and emotional wellbeing at risk. In that case, by all means go stoke the fires of resentment, anger, and disappointment. But if it's mutual cooperation, peace of mind, seasons of joy and family stability that you want, then always think before you speak or act.

Using the suggestions and tips here is a great start, but be prepared to do a lot more. Not only will you be able to create a positive co-parenting relationship with your Ex, you'll also experience personal growth while preserving your health and contributing in a meaningful way to your kids' lives.

I know that some of you may be asking *what if none of this works?* You have tried everything in your power to keep it classy and co-parent positively, but you just keep hitting a brick wall. Your situation still hasn't reached that healthy place. The other parent just can't seem to get it together for whatever reason. Or is it that you feel like your child is not in a safe environment? If you are continually up against impossible odds when dealing with your ex then you must do what's best for the kids. In these cases the court system might be your saving grace. Always remember that the best interests of your children is the overall goal

The Art of Compromise

Think Bold, Be Creative

I recently watched an episode of the HBO hit series, *Billions*. The storyline focused on one of the power couples, a state prosecutor and his wife, the executive employee business coach for a high-powered hedge fund corporation. I was particularly moved by the scene because the couple's children are roughly the same age as ours, between six and eight years old. Setting aside their professions, I'm using this example because I believe you too can relate to the scenario.

After she discovered that he'd jeopardized her career for his own political advancement, she told him she wanted him out of their house. Though he was truly remorseful and wanted to work it out at home, her justifiable anger was way too intense for any such consideration.

Once calm was restored however, they understood how much damage could be caused by interrupting the stability of their children's home life. This scene illustrated a point I made in the "The Sky Is Falling" chapter.

To the best of our ability we must make our children feel safe. I often repeat this. The TV couple agreed to a major adjustment, a new family system (he moved out of their home), but each of them would spend nights there with the kids. In other words, they split the time between them equally! By alternating sleepovers of three nights and four nights, the children would have one parent at home with them during all peak times.

It was a sudden but necessary shift from the norm. But the children weren't subjected to witnessing animosity between their mom and dad, which is always a big win! There was also a collateral benefit at play: subconsciously the children were learning two of life's greatest lessons, the art of compromise and teamwork. One of their parents is available to them for dinner, homework, playtime, breakfast, and listening time. The parents may not live together, but their children still bring their troubles and fears home to the two people who love them more than anything or anyone else in the world.

Even with the mature decisions carefully executed, children are still prone to confusion. They still want what they want, the family structure they've always known. When that's no longer possible, it's natural for them to want to blame one or the other parent for their changed circumstances. I love how the series writers tackled a conversation between the dad and the kids. I'm paraphrasing a little, but this is spot on with the essence of the conversation.

The Billions Episode: The children sat at the counter watching their dad chop vegetables for dinner. At a glance, the conversation appeared to be relaxed – but I recognized the undercurrent right away because I've experienced it with our two little darlings. It's the unspoken opinions hovering over their little heads, trapped in question bubbles waiting to burst free. Finally, the little girl expresses her wish for their mom to eat with them that night. Her brother, without skipping a beat, chimes in with "she doesn't want to." The dad then looks across at his children, feels their pain and uncertainty, then stops chopping and sets the knife on the counter.

"Look at me," he says, "look at me. That's not true. Your mom loves you, she always wants to be with you. I messed up, this is all on me. I know you kids look to us because we're the adults. You look at us and you think that we have it all together, but we don't. We make mistakes; I made a big mistake. It's not on you and it's not on her. Your mom loves you and so do I. But this situation, where we are now, this is on me. Okay?"

As the scene ended, I thought to myself, *wow*, that was powerful. I found myself wishing everyone would exercise that sort of objective logic under similar circumstances.

I can say beyond a shadow of a doubt that I'd speak up to defend my children's dad if they were to voice any doubt about his love for them, and I'm confident he'd do the same for me. Ready for your mind to be blown? I'm also certain that my children's stepmom would speak up on my behalf – and I'd certainly do the same for her. We're both moms, and we understand the importance of supporting one another. Our children are siblings, and whenever they spend time together, whether on the West Coast at their home or the East Coast at mine, our kids will feel at home. **This is the power of creating positive co-parenting relationships!**

Believe me, I know there will be no shortage of opportunities for heart-to-heart talks with your child. They do ask questions (and contrary to the opinions of some well-meaning friends and family), children deserve answers to their questions. It's the chance to be the best possible role model for them. Don't bother listing your Ex's shortcomings; that's his or her job. Yours is to seize the moment to teach your child the importance of personal accountability. The ability to conduct balanced self-reflection is a powerful character trait that will serve you well when redefining the relationship you have with your Ex. Watching and learning this self-reflection from you is a hugely important lesson that will serve your children well – for the rest of their lives. Our ability to pass that asset on to our children is just as important to their future happiness and health as nourishing their bodies with water and the right foods. And it's far more important than being able to buy them the most recent electronic game or trendy outfit.

Here's the thing – you can foster relationships together like this with your own blended family. All that is necessary is that you and your Ex to come to terms about the way you want to move forward.

How did we get here? By blocking and shutting out the barrage of negative unsolicited criticism *from people outside our lives*. It's hard enough for people who still enjoy their anonymity, but when celebrity is part of the mix, believe me, the challenges are increased exponentially! People meddle, choosing sides as if they have the right to judge you and your private family matters. Oddly enough, people who were friends with *both* of you somehow decide it's mandatory that they choose sides – it's a very rare human who will remain friends with both of you! Although it comes with the territory, the distraction can get crazy at times – and we were blessed with a few of those rare unicorns. Only those of us caught up in the public eye can fully grasp the magnitude of these challenges.

We're just like anyone else, really, we feel exactly the same emotions, joy, anger, sorrow, and pain. Nothing came easy in the beginning of our journey. To be perfectly honest, some of that outside interference did penetrate our spirit enough to warrant responses, not just to the privacy invaders, but to each other as well.

Still the three of us managed to rise to the occasion and do exactly what mature adults should do. We forged through the vicious commentary and the mischaracterizations. We redirected our energy, doubled down on individual career goals, and most important, focused the attention on shielding our children from external chaos.

It didn't happen overnight, mind you. Along the way, lots of stuff happened – there are so many paths that lead to more anxiety and confusion! But there comes a time when you must sit alone in quiet reflection to assess your entire situation and determine who the key players are and why they matter more than others.

No one is perfect, and we all make mistakes. It's okay, it's more than okay – it's normal! It's not the fall-down that determines our future. It's our ability to rise after we've fallen. It's how we get back up from the fall. It's how you rise up and carry on.

I firmly believe that there is a new version within each of us, a higher-self yearning to be set free. During my quiet time, I imagined my higher self, a copper-toned Wonder Woman, strong and wise beyond measure. Firmly, but gently, she told me that the life I desired was available as long as I didn't get in my own way. I've heeded that advice faithfully!

The moral of this is for you to reimagine your life, trying to be open to new ways of doing things. You've probably heard that "where you begin is not nearly as important as where you finish." I've been rocking that mindset – using it to get me from point A to point B – and I'm very pleased with the result. I encourage you to experience the very best version of who you were born to be ... a gifted, inspired, blessed spiritual being with infinite potential!

The Power of Self-Awareness

Knowing Why You Do What You Do

$\mathcal{F}$ ear can be our best friend or our worst enemy. The fight or flight instinct is natural; it instructs us to run from a grizzly bear rather than standing there imagining that it can be defeated with our bare hands. I don't know about you, but run like hell gets my vote!

This metaphor reminds me of why so many relationships either don't last, or remain stagnant for way too long. Fear of commitment or fear of letting go, whichever the case, is a prohibitor to experiencing complete satisfaction in your life.

Refusing to call it quits out of fear over what people will think and say is a ticket straight to misery. Clinging to a relationship that feels empty, simply because it's the devil you know, is a very poor choice. That mindset won't allow you growth or positive change – it will, in fact, block it.

The future holds so many delicious possibilities for you but the only way you will taste those possibilities is to step out of your comfort zone. Fear is a permanent companion for all of us in our lives.

Think of it as a franchise. No sooner do we conquer one fear, than another creeps up to take its place. We're defeated by it when we lack self-awareness. Once you figure that part out, you can learn how to negotiate with fear to secure the best deal for yourself.

Another sure way to stifle progress is to try to micro-manage your Ex's time with the children, such as inserting yourself into their time together by calling every ten minutes for a report on their whereabouts. That one, I'll admit, took me a while to get! Another is stubbornly refusing to accept that he's moved on with someone else who makes him happy. This is a tough one, I know. But let's face it, everyone deserves to be happy – and your Ex is no exception!

Life is seasonal. And change is the _only_ constant.

Other Baby Mama Drama

*L*et me say up front here that I realize I'm flirting with a hyper-sensitive, delicate, thorny, and seriously complicated issue in this section. I can't claim personal experience with this specific situation, though I've seen the negative impact it has on children. To my knowledge there's no tried-and-true method or step-by-step guide on the market that teaches anyone how to calmly navigate through the raw human emotions that erupt upon discovery that a spouse has fathered a child with another woman.

Seen the movie *Fences* with Denzel Washington? Viola Davis' portrayal of this emotional annihilation is superb.

Part of the mission of this book is to simply offer food for thought for healing. Ignoring this very real and complex relationship dilemma would have been a copout. If anything you read hits home for you personally, or for someone close to you, I only ask that you please try to keep an open mind and heart. Remind yourself that your overall goal is inner peace.

I'll jump in here with the assumption that you feel as I do about children – that they are little earth angels. Every child is born pure and innocent, open to giving and receiving love. We adults are supposed to be the guardians of their innocence.

I truly believe that our personal future will be determined by the way we treat the most vulnerable among us, children and of course our elders, and how fiercely we protect and lift them up. Unfortunately, too often children become one of the many moving targets caught in the crossfire of doomed relationships. Sometimes they even are thrown in the same basket along with friends and relatives who get blamed for being the meddling forces behind the breakup! The wrath-rod will strike anyone at any time, even unborn babies!

When infidelity is at the core of a breakup, civility and sanity vanish. All you can think is, he cheated and didn't use protection ... WTF! He cheated and risked infecting *you* with a sexually-transmitted disease! He's going to be *father* to another woman's baby. He cheated and now, ohmygod ohmygod ohmygod she's going to have his child, she's going to have his child, she's going to have his baby!!

You're hurt. You're beyond hurt. You're angry. In fact, you are wanna-die-right-now hurt and angry. No, wait, angry is such an understatement. What you are is 3000-pound raging bull, fuming from the nostrils, frothing at the mouth, blinded by rage and shock and revenge <u>LIVID</u>!!!

You close your eyes to block out his face and wind up envisioning their bodies entwined, which prompts the image of a hundred matadors waving red banners in front of you. And you know, you know beyond a shadow of a doubt, that if it's the last thing you do on this earth, you will grow horns to gorge them with, especially HER. No wait, especially HIM!

Irrational thoughts and craziness whirl inside your brain like funnel clouds of sand whipping around, swept up in the gale force winds of a monster tornado.

You could have eventually forgiven his cheating. Maybe. The affair could have been a turning point in your relationship, even an opportunity for the two of you to realize how much you truly love each other. Perhaps you'd even marry or renew your vows. You would have kept his transgression to yourself; no one needed to know.

But with a kid by another woman on the way, that coverup is no longer an option. You feel ashamed for his behavior (which on the surface makes no sense), but you do anyway. It's followed by the voice in your head screaming at ear-piercing level, "Just you wait!!! Payback's gonna be a bitch on steroids you mofo!"

You usually think of yourself as a good person, so you really don't want to resent a little person who weighs less than last year's Thanksgiving turkey, someone who had absolutely nothing whatsoever to do with your current agony – except for the fact this little person now *exists*. The same intense emotions apply if this is a toddler or teen child you're just finding out about years later. But, God help you you do, you *really resent that child* no matter what the age. It's illogical and unfair and you know it. But still.

As clouds of confusion eventually begin to clear away, you begin a different conversation with yourself, to some degree at least. You realize it's not the child you hate at all, it's HER. Yes, he's also to blame – there's no doubt he shoulda kept it in his pants. Together they've managed to near-drown you in shock and grief, to snuff out a light in your soul, and you're determined to find that light and turn it back on.

You want to tap into your higher self, the one you heard your pastor, or Deepak Chopra or someone talk about one time, or maybe it was Iyanla Vanzant. But you ain't there yet. Right now all you seem able to do is spit, grind your teeth, cuss and breathe fire, and stubbornly refuse to ever let that woman or her child anywhere near your child or children.

Why should you? She knew what she was doing. She knew he already had a family. She shoulda got her own damn man instead of bedding yours, the damn tramp. Well, you might say to yourself (you have lots of conversations with yourself), I hope she has a good job because "they" (her and her baby) aren't getting a dime of his money or your money. And don't even think about bringing that kid around to get child support or meet your kids!

But wait, it's his child and they're siblings ... *well that's just too damn bad!*

And so it begins. Yet another child, another little earth angel is banned, labeled an outcast, branded a bastard, inferior and shamed ... and unwanted.

I was unable to pinpoint a specific guide for this landmine, which of course dates back centuries. But, during my research for this project, I did come across quotes on children, like this one by the late former South African President Nelson Mandela, offering a perspective worthy of consideration.

"Our children are our greatest treasure. They are our future. Those who abuse them tear at the fabric of our society and weaken our nation." (National Men's March in 1997)

Before you shake your head in protest and mutter that Mr. Mandela's quote doesn't apply to you, please recall my little request at the beginning of the chapter ... all I asked is that you keep an open mind and heart. I would never suggest that a decision to not allow siblings to meet constitutes child abuse. However, what I hope to do is expand the conversation to reveal how this terrifically complicated family situation turns into a generational problem that ultimately haunts everyone in the future.

Maybe you can recall instances when you've felt unwanted, unloved, or unattractive? Well, it's not because you woke up some morning and decided you wanted to experience such dreadful feelings. It's likely because during your childhood, someone close to you (intentionally or not) made a remark in your presence that scarred your spirit. Many grownups are walking around still wounded, because of some rejection from the past. You may have shrugged it off at the time, or maybe not, but still it lingers in the subconscious mind, quietly coloring your decisions and influencing behavior.

There is a ton of disharmony and chaos within too many families and communities. A great deal of it stems from external forces, systemic racism, generational poverty, inadequate access to quality healthcare, inferior public schools, job discrimination – and other ills of our current culture. There are specific actions we can take to improve these circumstances, like pressuring policymakers into doing the right thing, and showing up to demand that schools provide our children with educational tools that will help them achieve excellence.

No question, there's already plenty of political activism afoot. We're in the streets, raising our voices in protest against police shootings, domestic violence, sexual assault, sex trafficking, employment issues, and more. Black women have always been on the frontline, winning battles against injustices that diminish our communities. We continue to blaze new trails while fighting unresolved battles. I'm so proud of young women like Alicia Garza, Patrisse Cullers, and Opal Tometi, who co-founded the Black Lives Matter movement in response to the killing of an unarmed teenager, Trayvon Martin. These young women and others like them have taken their cues from the warriors who came before them.

Harriet Tubman, Rosa Parks, Sojourner Truth, Ida B. Wells Barnett, Shirley Chisholm, Angela Davis – and countless others who sacrificed lives and livelihoods to ensure that the life of every Black woman, man, and child matters. Their primary struggle years ago focused on protecting our ancestors, especially children, from the hate-fueled danger all around them.

That makes me wonder today whether the rest of us are trying hard enough to honor those legacies. My feelings and thoughts are racing ahead, so please bear with me while I search for answers to questions seldom considered when grappling with the messy relationship quagmires that entrap children.

Haven't our children been the objects of hate long enough? Is it too idealistic to think we're capable of shielding them from feeling unloved, undervalued, and unwanted? (Surely they'll encounter plenty of haters to enthusiastically fill that role.) Is it too much to ask that we act as fearless allies for every child regardless of birth status? How high are you and I willing to rise above the noise when our faith is tested? Are you willing to push past the pain of betrayal for the sake of breaking the cycle of pain?

Should a man behave responsibly, keep it in his pants and/ or wrap it up? Hell yeah! Should she think upfront about all the consequences of bringing a child into the world with a man who already has a wife and family? Absolutely! But when two adults fail miserably at being responsible and respectful, is it then fair to punish an innocent child – and to prevent siblings from building a relationship with each other if they want to?

I have not come across a guide that teaches how to rise above our own disappointment, fear, and anger to embrace these earth angels. But I don't need anyone else to tell me what I already know, which is that *hurt people hurt other people*. I know that love, and not hate, is the answer to our collective healing. I know that we are the solution to many of our internal problems and that it's time to fix the things that are broken in us to give future generations a fighting chance.

Now is our time, not just to think outside the box, but also to destroy the box. It won't be easy, but you don't have to do it alone. Prayer is amazing, I wouldn't be standing today were it not for my devout faith in God and the power of prayer. However, I also believe that the God we serve guides the steps of men and women toward healing.

Two extraordinary women accepted an invitation to contribute their thoughts and professional advice on the topics discussed in this book. I hope you'll pay careful attention to what they have to say about the importance of knowing when it's time to reach for help – because it makes us stronger, not weaker. Because reaching out to the right people ends the suffering sooner and gets us closer to the healing we need faster.

You Are Not Superwoman!

My Body Cried Out

Contributed by Terrie M. Williams

*F*or several days I stayed in bed with the covers pulled over my head and the blinds drawn to block out even the tiniest glimmer of sunlight. I ignored the phone and the doorbell. I didn't want to see anyone's face or hear the sound of anyone's voice. I didn't want to talk or smile, or handle personal or business affairs. Not even the prescribed antidepressants I'd been taking for years relieved the weight I felt bearing down on my chest. I was at peace only when I slept, so naturally all I wanted to do was sleep – sleep and eat junk.

At the time I didn't realize it, but I had finally hit bottom. After all those years of wearing the mask, of sobbing myself to sleep at night, of using food to numb the pain, of losing myself in my PR business, representing clients and traveling around the globe for speaking engagements – my mind and my body were done. Both screamed *you are not Superwoman!* and then flatly refused to cooperate. The time had come to break my silence, to stop worrying about what people might say. I was already down, couldn't fall off the floor. The only way to go was up.

After long talks with both God and my therapist, I found the courage to share my story with the world. In 2005 *Essence* magazine ran it on the cover – Terrie M. Williams: "Depression and the Superwoman." Up till then, I'd truly felt alone. But when over 10,000 emails and letters came pouring in, I realized the depth of the crisis.

Suddenly the reasons so many people remained silent made perfect sense – most were just like me. I'd grown up surrounded by women and men who never uttered a word about feeling sad or blue. No way could they have escaped hardships they'd endured without experiencing mental anguish. They simply got up every day and did whatever it took to survive, provide for family and attempt to live with dignity, all while being rejected and disrespected by common enemies, racism, classism, and poverty.

Many of our foreparents found comfort in alcohol, which served to create even greater generational problems. As we look around us, it should be evident that we've inherited the scars and wounds of our mothers and fathers, same as they did from their parents. They didn't intentionally pass pain on to us – it's just the natural order of things.

I realize that the stigma associated with mental health issues remains a taboo topic, especially within Black communities. But there is an old saying, "When you know better, you do better."

The point of sharing my story in Monyetta's important book is two-fold. One, to remind you that "hurt people hurt other people." There could be times when you and your Ex are lashing out at each other, but the anger is misdirected, and you're just fighting old demons on new days. Two, to simply say this: to see a therapist as a family or an individual is a gift that will keep on giving. Understand that you are not crazy; it's not a copout and God won't be offended if you seek the help that gets to the root of your problems with anger, depression, fear, and anxiety. The truth is, God wants you and your family to be happy, healthy, and strong. God helps those who help themselves? It's true!

I sincerely hope that your eyes and heart are opened wider as you read through this book. I pray too, that you and your family find the peace and happiness you richly deserve.

Terrie M. Williams, author of
Black Pain: It Just Looks Like We're Not Hurting

Therapy Can Help Co-Parenting

Dr. Cynthia Grace

*L*et's face it – breaking up is hard to do. While some relationships do end amicably, many don't end by mutual consent. Frequently, one person wants to stay – or fix things – and the other person wants out.

Often, one or both in a relationship leave with baggage that remains unpacked for some time. When children are products of these relationships, breaking up results in added complications. These complications stem from the challenges inherent in having to restructure the relationships and interactions between the parents, and between the parents and their children. How this restructuring is handled brings into sharp focus the personal characteristics of the parents (good and bad), and their commitment to the wellbeing of their children.

Most of our learning about how to be a parent is informal. We typically do not take parenting classes nor attend parenting workshops before we have children. Our first lessons usually come from the people who raise us. We learn to trust others to care for us – or we learn to mistrust or doubt that care and safety will be there when we need it. Our parents help shape our awareness of our strengths and weaknesses, or they fail to do so. Our parents help teach us how to love maturely or how to not love at all.

A huge dose of our sense of self-worth often comes from what parents communicate to us about our value. How people parent is often a function or direct reflection (like it or not!) of how they were parented, and even how their parents were raised. Many times, parenting successes and failures end up being passed on from generation to generation.

Perhaps the most important lessons learned from those who parent us relate to our ability to manage emotions. How we express feelings, and how we cope with feelings, are both shaped by our experiences with those charged with nurturing, guiding, and protecting us. It is not an accident that when we need to calm down, we resort to the thoughts, expressions, tones, and non-verbal behaviors we observed coming from those around us. This is precisely why our adult relationships end up replicating our parents' relationship. This partially explains why some children grow up feeling loved, respected, and cared for, while others grow up feeling unvalued and neglected.

Most of the mistakes parents make, of course, are unintentional. Through faulty learning, they may be unaware that a particular approach to parenting could have long-term negative effects. I think of the many adults I have met who said they were negatively affected by their separated parents who were not on the same page when it came to raising them. Many say that they were vicariously traumatized as a result of witnessing emotionally and physically abusive interactions between their parents. Some are hurt by the negative statements that one parent makes about the other. Some children end up feeling like pawns or weapons used by one parent to manipulate, control, or punish the other.

You probably have heard all the reasons that people who really need therapy avoid it like the plague. Admittedly, the decision to see a therapist is not easy for many people. First of all, the decision requires that we admit to ourselves, and to someone else, that we need help. This admission may not correspond with how we see or would like to see ourselves. So many people think that admitting the need for therapy is an admission of weakness or "craziness" or desperation.

Denial that a problem exists is among the biggest reasons those who need therapy do not seek it. It is not uncommon for some people who really need therapy to consciously or unconsciously block awareness that a problem exists. This can happen when dysfunctional behaviors are believed to be normal because of childhood or familial experiences these individuals were repeatedly exposed to. This can also happen when a person is aware that there is a problem, but is invested in maintaining the problem for reasons such as a need for control or power.

Some even believe that seeking help from a therapist is indicative of a lack of faith in God. Consequently, they will not avail themselves of psychotherapy because they view psychotherapy as a betrayal of their religion. They internalize statements like "come on, you don't need therapy" or "Just bring it to God" or "Pray and everything will be all right." Prayer is powerful and may be all that is needed in some cases. But in some other cases it should be combined with therapy.

Trust in the value of therapy will influence our willingness to accept this form of help, along with beliefs about the therapist's potential, and even our available time and other resources. In order to receive help from a therapist, we must make contact with a trained person who is likely someone with whom we are unfamiliar. Therapy requires that we commit to a structured relationship with that person and talk openly about our lives, past and current struggles, how we manage our emotions, and how we behave in various situations.

Lack of knowledge about the process and potential of therapy, mistrust, and the cost are key reasons that the decision to seek therapy is not easy to make. Many of us have been socialized to *not* talk to people we don't know about the intimate details of our lives. This bit of socialization may serve as a barrier to the willingness to seek psychotherapeutic assistance. It's a strange idea – being in a professional relationship that is not a friendship, but requires that one person relate to the other with open, honest self-disclosure. Yet the one-sided nature of the relationship is a very important aspect of the therapeutic alliance, and is a key element in the successful outcome of the therapy.

Because of our country's history of ethnic and race relations, the long-time lack of black and brown health care providers, and the persistent disparities in the quality of the care provided based on race, people of color often have some "cultural mistrust" in professionals who are culturally different. As a result, many believe it unlikely that a racially or culturally different therapist can understand them and provide them with good care. Some are even concerned that the professional relationship that is supposed to be helpful could even be harmful because of racism, stereotyping, or some other type of social bias. Even when therapists and clients are both from similar sociocultural backgrounds, the trust is not automatic. One of the biggest sources of reluctance to seek therapy is the strongly held belief by many that "you don't put your business out there because you just can't trust people."

The stigma associated with needing therapy is quite strong in some communities – and with some cultural or religious backgrounds. In fact, mental illness and the need for therapy commonly are taboo topics in the Black community. I have often heard the statement that "Black folks don't need therapy ... therapy is for crazy White people." Also, many people of different sociocultural backgrounds have misconceptions about what therapy is, and are not confident that it will be helpful. They may want to avoid embarrassment, or are afraid of what might be "uncovered."

When therapy is needed – or even just *useful* – to support healthy co-parenting, and one or both parties are reluctant, it is not uncommon to hear comments like "I don't need that, I am not the crazy one" or "a therapist can't tell me what to do" or "this is what she wanted, so this is what she gets." Or even "I am not going to be nice to him and I don't need him and some therapist to tell me how to raise my child." Far too often, anger and resentment guide behavior. Unfortunately, as a result, dysfunctional behaviors are used to express underlying feelings. In other words, people "act out" or "act up."

Grief and depression over the breakup will affect the parents, the children, or both. Grief is a natural reaction to loss, and people react to loss in different ways. However, when loss affects a person's ability to function for an extended period, and is accompanied by extreme sadness and withdrawal, therapy should be considered. Some people when depressed become very irritable and uncooperative. These symptoms often interfere with the quality of the communication that is essential for good parenting and co-parenting.

Children may experience difficulty sleeping, poor concentration, lowered school performance, or bed-wetting. Behavioral changes seemingly unrelated to family relationships may well be triggered by grief or stress about the breakup. Children may also react to the separation of their parents by being oppositional, rebellious, and defiant. These are signs that counseling may be advisable or even necessary. Thoughts or any indication of preoccupation with suicide should be addressed immediately with the assistance of a mental health professional.

Therapy assists co-parents in growing into a successful co-parenting role in a way that fosters the healthy development of their children. At the root of poor co-parenting are poorly managed emotions, inadequate knowledge, and perhaps a deficiency in the maturity that good co-parenting requires.

The mature parent is committed to making the needs of the child primary. The mature parent understands that children need stability, predictability, and guidance. Mature parents understand the importance of a healthy bond between both parents – and they work together to achieve it.

The initial focus of co-parenting therapy is the assessment of the barriers to high quality co-parenting. The assessment will provide an understanding of the factors that predisposed the couple to parenting problems, the factors that precipitated the current problems, and the behaviors, feelings, and perspectives that are maintaining the problems in co-parenting. Strategies for learning and maintaining effective parenting is explored during the therapy process, and guidance is provided for implementing those strategies.

Finding the right therapist is key to ensuring the best possible outcomes. The therapist should be someone with whom both parties are comfortable. A therapist should be experienced, able to understand the issues from the appropriate cultural perspective, be non-judgmental and able to build consensus. A good therapist is also skilled in de-escalation techniques. Keep in mind that therapists are diverse with respect to education and training. They may be Psychologists, Licensed Clinical Social Workers, Licensed Mental Health Counselors, or Licensed Marriage and Family Therapists.

I am often asked about the difference between psychiatrists and psychologists. Both are referred to as "doctors" and spend roughly the same number of years preparing for their professions. However, psychiatrists hold medical degrees and are trained to prescribe medication. Psychologists, on the other hand, hold PhD's and are considered experts in diagnosing and treating mental health problems with psychological tools including but not limited to psychological testing and therapy for individuals, groups, families, and couples. Psychologists do not prescribe medication, but rely instead on a wealth of knowledge about non-medication options for ameliorating psychological distress.

Ask your primary care practitioner for a referral, and ask any of your friends co-workers or family members who might have recommendations. Do not hesitate to look online for assistance in finding a therapist, or for information about therapists you are considering. The widely distributed publication *Psychology Today* has an excellent online tool for locating licensed therapists nationwide.

Paying for therapy places an added demand on our resources. Fees vary as a function of the therapist's discipline and experience, the type of therapy requested, and the setting. Some therapists charge a fee for an initial consultation, while others do not. Some therapists will charge fees on a sliding scale tied to what you are able to pay. The cost of therapy should never be a source of financial stress, so discuss payment openly and honestly. If you can, use your health insurance. To avoid increasing your stress, do not commit to paying more than you can afford. For an affordable option, consider a community mental health center with experienced and culturally competent therapists.

I was attracted to the field of Psychology because it appeared to offer an opportunity to do something with a high degree of relevance and career satisfaction. The chance to have positive impact on the lives of people and the wellbeing of groups and communities of people who are important to me is priceless. I have never, for one minute, regretted my decision to become a Licensed Clinical Psychologist. I am grateful for what I have been able to give as a result of this amazing profession, and the impact it has had on my life and my family's health and wellbeing. The opportunity for guided self-exploration has given me many gifts. I wish the same for you.

Dr. Cynthia Grace, Psychotherapist

You Are Unstoppable

Get Fit, Focused, Fierce - Ready for Anything

I try to work out at least four days a week, except for Sunday, which is reserved for family. Whether at the gym or at home, I maintain my commitment to a fit and healthy lifestyle.

It's not easy. I'm a full-time mom of two small children. After I drop them off at school, I'm on my workout grind. Keeping this promise makes me feel good about myself. I know I'm not shortchanging myself.

This fuels my confidence, and keeps me motivated and determined to accomplish my goals. How can we raise healthy children if we're not leading by example? It might not always seem like it, but kids do take their cues from us. Sure, there's plenty of outside influence too, which is why it's so important that they see us putting our best foot forward.

The same applies to our children and their happiness. We can't expect them to have a positive outlook on life if we're walking around projecting doom and gloom. Do as I say, not as I do just doesn't work. I say this knowing full well that it's seldom easy. But I also know that doing the things that are in our own best interest and our children's best interests is worth every bit of our effort.

This following chapter isn't about why you and the kids' dad shouldn't badmouth each other in front of them – I'll assume that's clear. It's also not about scheduling visitation, or junk-food taboos, or house rules. It isn't about how incredibly cunning children are – how our sweet little mischiefmakers quickly seize opportunities to manipulate situations in their favor.

This is about YOU time. I realize this might seem contrary to what you've been told, but it's okay to disregard old ways of thinking that don't serve your growth. The truth is, when you take care of yourself, everyone wins. Consider this section of the book as a clarion call for you to get fit, focused, fierce, and unstoppable.

Women are notorious for placing our personal needs on the back burner. Whether it's not getting enough rest, not treating yourself to a massage, or not making time to meditate – somehow you end up on some future to-do list.

Unfortunately the large majority of women are self-neglect practitioners. Prioritizing the needs of others above our own health and wellbeing is practically programmed into our DNA. And that must change.

Part of the problem is that we've been pre-conditioned to believe it's selfish to address our own needs first – or at all. Very little if any thought went into the consequences of ignoring our health. Bottom line, the entire family structure, the day-to-day operation, is threatened when our health fails. That is the reasoning behind my position on women being the epicenter of family, culture, and community.

We're at even greater risk now than before; there are so many additional demands on our time and energy. I'm not suggesting that the women before us had it a single iota easier, in fact we'll never know the level of pain and struggle endured by our grandmothers and their parents before them. They were subjected to the harshest demands over their time and bodies. Still, against the backdrop of those hardships, they managed to give the best of themselves to our parents! They deserve no less than our gratitude, love, and respect for their immeasurable sacrifices.

Women today are constantly spinning multiple plates in the air. Our lives and commitments are spread over broader geographic territories, making it all the more difficult to get everything accomplished the same day.

Communities aren't the same either. Gone are the days in most areas where neighbors plan to settle down for generations. We live in a society that is far more transient.

People buy houses for the purpose of flipping them, or they move on to better deals. Almost no one works in the same job for 20 or 30 years now. This all means that family members who used to provide childcare are no longer right next door or down the street, and daycare (who used to do that?) is located miles away from our homes. Parents living in urban areas use public transportation to drop off their kids and pick them up on their way home.

Our careers are way more demanding, oftentimes requiring out-of-town travel. It's not just the women executives who are stretched thin – hourly employees work much longer too. The last time I checked there's still only 24 hours in a day. We have only two hands, two feet, two eyes and ears. We have one brain, one heart, and one body.

This section of the book is your call to action – it's meant to urge you off that back burner! Step out from the back of the line and march straight to the front of it. It's all about you becoming laser-focused on your journey forward, increasing self-awareness and probing your psyche. I won't apologize for any repetitious instruction that might help you experience a real breakthrough. We're undoing a lifetime of bad habits and misguided beliefs that haven't served our growth, so we must be vigilant.

When I first started my healing journey, I spent a great deal of time reconnecting with my inner light. The work required my undivided attention, which wasn't easy between my children and a slew of other distractions. Still,

I understood the importance of having some ME time. The math was easy: set aside at least one of the 24 hours for myself. In time, I was able to identify more pockets of time that I could treat myself to. I was determined to strike a sensible balance including good mom, healthy woman, being social, and living as an entrepreneur. I also stepped outside my comfort zone and became more open to different perspectives.

After having my second child I wasn't happy with my body weight or my mood. I needed to make some changes and I don't mean superficial changes – some were downright radical.

Here are a few statistics I pulled together for you from the American Heart Association's website.

- Cardiovascular diseases and stroke cause one in three women's deaths each year, killing a woman every 80 seconds.
- Cardiovascular diseases are the leading cause of death for African American women, killing over 48,000 annually.
- Hispanic women are likely to develop heart disease 10 years earlier than Caucasian women.
- Of African American women ages 20 and older, 48.3 percent have cardiovascular disease. Yet only 14 percent believe that cardiovascular disease is their greatest health problem.

There is wisdom in the old adage, "An ounce of prevention is worth a pound of cure." Exercising 30 minutes a day, five days a week, improves heart health and helps reduce the risk of heart disease. Other life-threatening illnesses are also kept at bay when you exercise.

I've stayed on the path of healing and forgiveness because I'm determined to be the best version of myself – the best mom for my two amazing children, and for myself. If there's one thing I know for sure it's that the better we are for ourselves, the better we are for our children. You have lots of time, energy and love to give, so make sure you're included!

Food-mood, Muscle, Motivation

Contributed by Terahshea J. McCray

*H*ave you ever stopped to question your daily mood swings? Most people don't. One minute you're feeling pretty good, the next you've slipped into an unexplainable funk, like self-loathing, self-doubt, or just general orneriness. Unless a mental health professional has diagnosed you with something serious like depression, you should probably start paying close attention to your food choices, because the foods you eat affect your moods. At the end of this chapter, I'll give you a short list of online resources where you can take your time to process information and, I hope, take this seriously. I'm going to cover exercise and how you can apply the benefits from it to build your positive co-parenting relationship.

Whether you have toddlers, 'tweens, or teens, being a parent requires loads of physical energy, endurance, patience, and mental clarity. That's a very tall order, especially if you're in crisis mode. All the more reason that exercise and eating the right foods should be at the top of your list.

It's typical for major life events such as a divorce, death, or loss of income to drain your brain, body, and spirit. Tempting as it may be to climb into bed, pull the covers over your head, and hide from the world, now is not the time to do it. It is time to guard yourself against the depression and anxiety that will rob you – and your children – of all the best life has to offer.

During this very vulnerable phase, it's crucial for you to drag yourself to a gym, go for a run, lift weights, ride a bike, roller skate, swim, or just sprint up and down your own staircase as if your life depended on it. Because it does.

Too many people buy into the prescription drug myth. That's a very slippery slope, one that you don't want to end up on. The temporary relief you might experience from taking a pill can't hold a candle to 20 minutes of vigorous physical exercise.

I've been a certified personal trainer and nutritionist since 1995. Over the span of my professional career I've trained people from all different walks of life. Whether they've been athletes, academics, single moms, celebrities, recovering addicts or Fortune 500 CEO's, exercise was the common denominator and the tool they used for accomplishing their desired goals.

In my personal and professional experience, I can say that the one thing that can shift you from feeling helpless, anxious, and uninspired is exercise. There's no doubt that our bodies can be a physical manifestation of the way we feel. Our mood changes based on the way we look. You can be fit, fine, and fabulous. Or not. Your toned and healthy body can keep you up and energetic even when faced with a herd of obstacles. Or not. You can have a beautiful home, a luxury car, and a swagger-worthy career, but if you're dissatisfied with your appearance or feel sluggish all the time, life can seem downright depressing.

Let's take two client examples; the names have been changed. First we have upwardly mobile Laura. On the surface her life seemed perfect – a beautiful home, dream car, and a very stable career brimming with growth potential. But Laura also had a major problem; she was very unhealthy. She was 75 lbs. overweight, her knees hurt like hell, she had tremendous back pain, and she hated looking in a mirror. Her body was a constant source of her physical and emotional pain. She dreaded family time because being around people required way too much energy for her to be fully present. She made excuses as often as possible, opting to stay home instead.

This was Laura's vicious cycle, and she ate all the wrong foods to cover the pain of her current life and her childhood traumas. The extra weight made her feel sluggish, which deepened her sadness, which made her eat and sleep more.

But Laura's journey turned upward when she decided to prioritize her health. By her own acknowledgement she's never felt as good about herself as she does now. She attributes this to her newfound ability to do pull-ups, squats, and planks. She talks about how great strength training makes her feel. That's because it gives her a sense of power, stability, and balance.

I'm proud of the progress she's made, but more important, Laura is proud of herself. She's in a much better place emotionally and physically. She knows the common denominator with her mood, muscle, and motivation is exercise. And she's also crystal-clear about why her back and knees aren't pain-ridden like before and diabetes is no longer a threat. I'm prone to repeat to my clients often, your health is your wealth – that's not some tired old cliché. It's the truth.

Our second case example is Erica. When we first met, she was 40, and I began preparing her to compete in a fitness show. This woman was jovial, committed to her physique, and recovering from heartbreak. Her life had been unexpectedly thrown off course. She didn't have the shiny new car in her driveway that she'd planned to purchase because her Ex had tapped into her savings and bought himself a new car. She didn't have a sparkling credit score anymore, either. But most of all, she didn't have the family life that she'd worked so hard to build.

Erica was a wreck until she decided that she was going to make some serious changes. She wanted to build a strong and toned body, so she adopted strength as the central theme for her new life. She wanted to be strong for her kids and her career – and most of all herself.

Lifting weights ignited a creativity that seemed to have been hidden in her soul. She became much more active as a parent; she planned day trips, picnics, and beach outings. This isn't surprising – weight training creates an adrenaline rush that releases dopamine into the brain. It's a natural high that clears away brain fog. The energy radiates from you so naturally that you aren't even aware of the effect unless you miss a few days of training, and then you notice that you feel a bit off-kilter.

You don't have to run yourself into the ground when you are training to improve your lifestyle. The goal is to "stimulate not annihilate" your body.

I'm a hands-on dad, and I know parenting requires acute mental clarity and physical stamina. It's only a matter of time until you experience some form of burnout or worse; you must set aside time to check off at least two of these from your list: exercise regularly, meditate, practice yoga, and maintain a healthy diet.

Customizing Your Body Transformation

When it comes to exercising to change your body, it's important to not compare your progress with anyone else's. Consider two women, Jalesa and Karen. They each weigh

170 pounds and have decided to start dieting and exercising together. According to Jalessa's plan for them, she and Karen will exercise four days a week. They'll start the "low-no carb diet." Their program consists of a 45-minute 1½-mile walk, three days a week, with one day of light lifting and another day of Pilates.

After four weeks, Jalesa is down to 160 pounds while Karen is down to 167 pounds. Why has Jalesa lost 10 pounds while Karen lost just three pounds? The simple answer – it's a matter of bio-cellular individuality as it relates to the oxidative and metabolic type of these carbon life forms. They are slow oxidative and fast oxidative, and therefore require opposing stimuli to the musculoskeletal system.

Huh? What this means is that Karen's approach must be completely different from Jalessa's. Why? Because Jalessa is probably slow-twitch dominant, meaning she is built for endurance. Karen, on the other hand, may be fast-twitch dominant, or built for strength, speed, and power. Consider these three key points:

Jalesa does well with 45-minute walks. Karen may need to start with 20-minute walks at a much faster pace.

Jalesa is fine using weights one day a week, completing two sets of each exercise for 15-20 reps. Karen needs at least three days of strength training where she is working hard to push out 8-12 reps per set.

Jalesa feels great on a high-protein diet, but by comparison, Karen is often tired and moody on this low-no carb diet. That's why she sneaks in some chocolate when Jalessa's not looking.

The bottom line is, if your program isn't working for you in four weeks, you should make a change or two. Jalesa chose a plan that worked for her genetic type.

How do you find the program that's right for you? The truth is, it's trial and error. You can try things on your own and monitor your progress. But a qualified personal trainer can assess your type sooner and help you reach your desired goal more efficiently.

Below are some resources that explain how and why foods affect your mood and overall health.

- Mood Food: Can What you Eat Affect Your Happiness?
  Health Line: bit.ly/2jDcKND

- 6 Ways Food Affects Your Mood
  Everyday Healthy: bit.ly/2kenjGq

- Nutritional Psychiatry: Your Brain on Food
  Harvard Health Blog: bit.ly/2uEulrk

If you want a book that provides a detailed look at at the topic, I recommend *The Food-Mood Connection:*

Nutrition-based and Environmental Approaches to Mental Health and Physical Wellbeing by Gary Null.

If you combine and apply what you learn about foods and nutrition to the benefits derived from exercise, you'll be empowered to lead the unstoppable life that is out there waiting for you!

Terahshea J. McCray
Personal Trainer CSCS, CPT & Nutritionist

It Does Take a Village

Family, Friends, Neighbors Need Each Other

*W*e're living in a very provocative time right now, a time of severe social, political, economic, and racial unrest. It's extremely important that we do everything we can to minimize family drama and to eliminate violence in our homes and communities. Having to pay close attention to everything happening around us all the time can be exhausting and overwhelming. When I was growing up, my parents didn't have to think about the possibility of a student bringing an automatic rifle (or even a gun) to school – but my generation does!

I don't mean for this closing chapter to feel heavy; forgive me if it does. What I really want is to emphasize the importance of our getting back to a village mindset. You know, when neighbors looked out for the neighbors' children and each other. Let's face it, once our babies start preschool, we're at the mercy of the people working there. We expect them to not only teach and feed our kids, but also protect them from harm. Even though you know there are really good people in the schools who would do their best in a crisis situation, you still feel uneasy. All the more reason for parents to get along with each other and for family members to be supportive.

It's never acceptable to advise a father to neglect his children. Ever. Yet some "friends" and relatives do it all the time. Shaffer touched on this in his foreword for the book. There are countless stories out there about relatives whispering in a man's ear to discourage his cooperation with his children's mother – including some people who once masqueraded as friends, but now try to use their influence to block any degree of possible peace between you and your Ex. Let's be clear, they do not have your children's best interest at heart, period.

My kids are truly blessed and so am I. Shaffer's mom Loraine is a true blessing in our lives. I'm eternally grateful to her for all her love and her ongoing support. She helps me stay sane! Shaffer lives full-time in Los Angeles, and his professional schedule keeps him super busy. Loraine is always there for us, and the kids love going to their granny's house on some weekends along with his sister Nicole – which is great because they get to play with their cousin Liam! My parents live in Louisiana and we get to visit only two or maybe three times a year, so having Loraine so close by is a true godsend. I love that our children get to experience a great relationship between their mom and their dad's mom.

Years ago, so many parents yearned to make life better for their children's sake. For most, it meant ending a cycle of financial struggle and providing for them in ways that their own parents couldn't afford while they were growing up. Now, the vision must also include a willingness to break certain cycles of secrecy and shame, cycles that have allowed the number of victims and violators to increase over the years. We have to hold ourselves and others accountable for actions. We need to get on the same page about the kind of world-community we want for our children and for future generations.

Every child deserves to attend schools where bullying isn't tolerated. Every girl should feel safe and be safe in the presence of boys and men, and young boys should be surrounded by responsible adult men who know the difference between right and wrong – and live it.

I really hope the things I've shared here will help you. Earlier I pointed out that there are no one-size strategies for developing positive co-parenting relationships. Trial and error are our teachers. The trick is keeping the learning curve as brief as possible so we can get on with the business of raising healthy, happy children.

Remember – and remind yourself – to surround yourself and your children with reasonable, fair-minded people. It does indeed take a village to raise a child ... popularized in the U.S. in 1996 by Hillary Clinton in her book of the same name, the saying is a Nigerian proverb that's common in many African languages. *It means that the upbringing of a child is not a solo act or even a parental endeavor – it's a communal effort.* Focus on the family and friends who not only have your back, but also are wise enough to keep their eyes on the prize, i.e. what's best for your children. Turn to the people who understand that it does indeed take a village to raise a child!

Resources for assistance

ARTICLES

- *Psychology Today*: Do's & Don'ts of Compassionate Parenting
- *Woman's Day*: Things Children of Divorce Wish Their Parents Wouldn't Do
- *Huffington Post*: How to Be a Hero to Your Children When Divorce Is Your Enemy

WEBSITES

- American Heart Association
- Centers for Disease Control and Prevention

BOOKS

- *Black Pain: It Just Looks Like We're Not Hurting* by Terrie M. Williams

- *Tears To Triumph: The Spiritual Journey from Suffering to Enlightenment* by Marianne Williamson
- *Healthy Women Rock: How to Live the Life You Desire and Deserve, Lose Weight & Control Negative Thoughts* by Madeline McCray & Terahshea McCray

Postscript

I dedicate this book to my dear brother,
the late Michael Wayne Shaw, Jr.

*D*eep in my heart you'll forever be my charismatic, smart, funny, big brother! You'll always be the super-talented one in the family, who taught his little sister how to dance and how to rap. Memories of the songs we created together as children have always been and will always be a source of inspiration behind my creative endeavors, especially music. I'll never forget your love of fishing, or the way you'd take my hand to bring me along while you and Rico caught bass, or how I watched you both as I toiled away, perfecting my mud pies. We had many adventures in the good ol' country ... priceless memories that will never fade! You taught me how to protect and defend myself when I was a young – lessons that prepared me for womanhood.

You were there for me in countless ways during my darkest hours. The sound of your voice during those late-night phone calls to check on me and the kids helped get me through that fire. You reminded me that I was a great mom, daughter, sister, and friend, and that I deserved the very best that life had to offer. You made me laugh through the tears and I'd hang up feeling a sense of pride and peace. I'd give the world to have known how to do the same for you.

When I first told you of my plans to write a book to help parents explore ways to cooperate with one another for the sake of their children, you praised me for always keeping it classy. You told me to always shine my light, and I promised you that I would. I am so grateful for the time that we had together and I will cherish it always. Thanks for letting us love on you as long as you did. I am so glad that you were surrounded by our loving family in the end and that you told us many times how much you loved and appreciated us.

Never in my wildest dreams could I have imagined you'd be gone by the time this book was published. Losing you has deepened the meaning of my promise; I want everyone to know that, more often than not, suicidal thoughts escalate. We must all be more vigilant and aware of the warning signs, because those signs often won't be obvious. According to a 2016 report by the Centers for Disease Control and Prevention (CDC), suicide was the second leading cause of death among individuals between the ages of 10 and 34, and the fourth leading cause of death among individuals between the ages of 35 and 54.

Unlike episodes of feeling blue, clinical depression is dangerous. The pain experienced every day by people living with depression is very, very real. It is the monster lurking in the shadows of the mind. Leaders in Black communities must do more to educate people about this condition. We are a faith-based people, and rightfully so. Our faith has kept us strong in ways that mattered to our very survival in a hostile land. But it's dangerous to think that depression or other brain disorders can be prayed away – these conditions must be brought before God AND a qualified therapist or psychiatrist. I'm well aware of the inhuman experimentation we've endured throughout the dark history of medicine under the guise of psychiatric advancement. These are very legitimate reasons for our suspicion. But we're also intelligent people with access to the internet. We can do the necessary homework to identify credible professionals who enter the field of medicine to heal, not harm us. Mental illness is a disease; it shouldn't be treated as a dirty secret, a spiritual punishment, or a moral weakness.

Yes, this acknowledgment belongs to my dear brother Michael. However, I'm also speaking for him because he's no longer here to do it. I'm writing this for men like Michael, many of whom are fathers struggling to make sense of their feelings, and many women, some of whom are mothers suffering in silence.

And I'm speaking to *you*, as you read my words here. I'm asking you to please pay close attention to your loved ones whose behavior might baffle you. Watch the women and teens in your life closely; sometimes that behavior is a cry for help that they can't bring themselves to ask for. Many times they're suffocated by unnecessary shame passed along by misguided beliefs, taboos, or outdated stigmas that have often resulted in deadly consequences. It's time to break any cycle of grief that can be avoided. Although there's no perfect time to begin breaking a cycle, I suggest that the end of an intimate relationship is as good a place to start as any.

I miss my brother so much. I know he's watching over me just like he did when we were little, only now he's an angel with a whole lot more swagger. Rest peacefully my dear brother! I LOVE YOU beyond infinity and I will always be your little sister!

Love, Monyetta

Acknowledgments

To my parents Michael Shaw Sr. and Linda B. Shaw – thank you for laying the strong foundation that enables me to be an unbreakable, unstoppable woman. You've always reminded me where my strength comes from – that no matter what, God has me. I love you Mommy and Daddy.

**My amazing grandmothers, Granny Emerline Bradford and the late Ester Ree Cheatham, attended all of my performances, pageants, plays, and sports events, and my love and appreciation for them is indescribable.

**My precious M's, Madilyn and Mason Shaw-Smith. You two show me the true meaning of unconditional love each and every day. You are my reasons! Every day on this earth I strive to be the best example for you – I pray that I will continue to make you proud. I love you beyond words, my Madi & Maso.

**Thank you to Shaffer (Ne-Yo) Smith, Madeline McCray, Terrie Williams, Terahshea McCray, and Cynthia Grace for your invaluable contributions to this project.

**To my awesome family, my spiritual advisors, life coaches, my pastor, and my amazing friends ... thanks for always being there. I love you all so very much!

About the Author

Monyetta Shaw was born in Shreveport, Louisiana, on May 31, 1980. A multi-talented young mogul and style maven, she's tugged at the heartstrings of Americans as they've fallen in love with her dedication to family, philanthropy, and fashion, along with her down-home Southern upbringing.

Monyetta's rise to fame began at an early age in her hometown of Shreveport as she embarked upon an entertainment and acting career after graduating from Louisiana Tech with a bachelor's in psychology. She is a member of Alpha Kappa Alpha and has a strong background in radio. At the young age of 19 she was the co-host of the popular "Daddy Roe Show."

Monyetta believes her most important role is being a mother to her two M's, Madilyn Grace and Mason Evan. It was from their middle names she decided to name her company The Evan Grace Group – a development, management, and publishing company.

Monyetta was honored with the Philanthropist of the Year Award by Beyond the Game Foundation. She partnered with the organization to build an orphanage in Swaziland Africa, and was recognized as *Rolling Out* Magazine's Top 25 Influential Women in Atlanta. She also supports the Compound Foundation, Kamp Kizzy, Boys and Girls Clubs of America, The League of Women Voters, and The National Black Arts Festival, and she serves on the advisory board of The Institute for Global Outreach; she currently takes care of 15 children every month in Ethiopia – for the past two years and counting.

Keep It Classy is Monyetta's third book. Her first, *The Adventures of Maddie*, is a children's book series begun in 2013; she's working on her second and third in the series, *Mysteries of Mason* and *Maddie and Mason Off to School*. Her most recent book, *Bigger than Me*, is full of motivation and inspiration from the heart.

Monyetta strives to live by one of her favorite scriptures, *Luke 12:48* – "To whom much is given, from that person much is expected," exemplified in her dedication to family, philanthropy, and business.

MonyettaShaw.com